WHEN UNICORNS TURN BAD

I'm so horny!

summersdale

Brody Jackson

WHEN UNICORNS TURN BAD

An Hachette UK Company
www.hachette.co.uk

Summersdale Publishers Ltd
Part of Octopus Publishing Group Limited
Carmelite House
50 Victoria Embankment
LONDON
EC4Y 0DZ
UK

www.summersdale.com

Printed and bound in China

ISBN: 978-1-78783-023-3

Substantial discounts on bulk quantities of Summersdale books are available to corporations, professional associations and other organisations. For details contact general enquiries: telephone: +44 (0) 1243 771107 or email: enquiries@summersdale.com.

Introduction

The glittery veil has been lifted, the rainbow mists are parted and the mystery is over: unicorns are mad, bad and dangerous to know! Their sugary sweet appearance and syrupy 'you do you' sentiments are a façade. They're just a herd of sherbet-sniffing horses, who like nothing more than to make trouble and poop rainbows.

Shield your eyes as the unicorns hoof it down the pastel path to depravity...

Let's make little grey unicorns together.

WHAT A BEAST!

Fancy pants

Spent the rent money on a new weave and I've got *no regrets*.

Nothing like
a sea wee.

U OK, hun?

SHE'S IN IT FOR THE DRAMA

I've come to the Enchanted Forest to see if I can get some

ENCHANTED BUSH.

#NOFILTER

#ALLNATURAL

PHOAR!

THE RUMOURS ARE TRUE – I'M ONE

dirty beast.

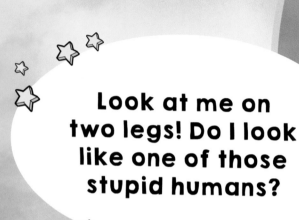

#AESTHETIC

MAGIC HOVER-FART

AWKWARD LEVEL:
your hairdresser does this and you say, 'I love it, thanks!'

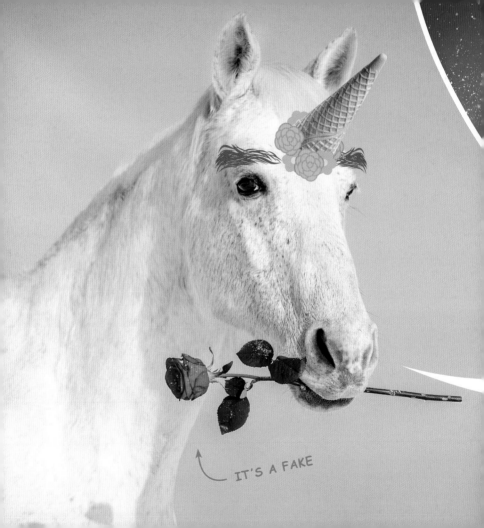

IT'S A FAKE

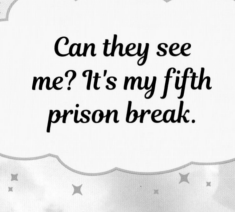

Can they see me? It's my fifth prison break.

I CAN SEE HIM

Everyone loves the effect when I burst out of the mist but no one talks about all this waiting around in the fog.

SO DRAMATIC!

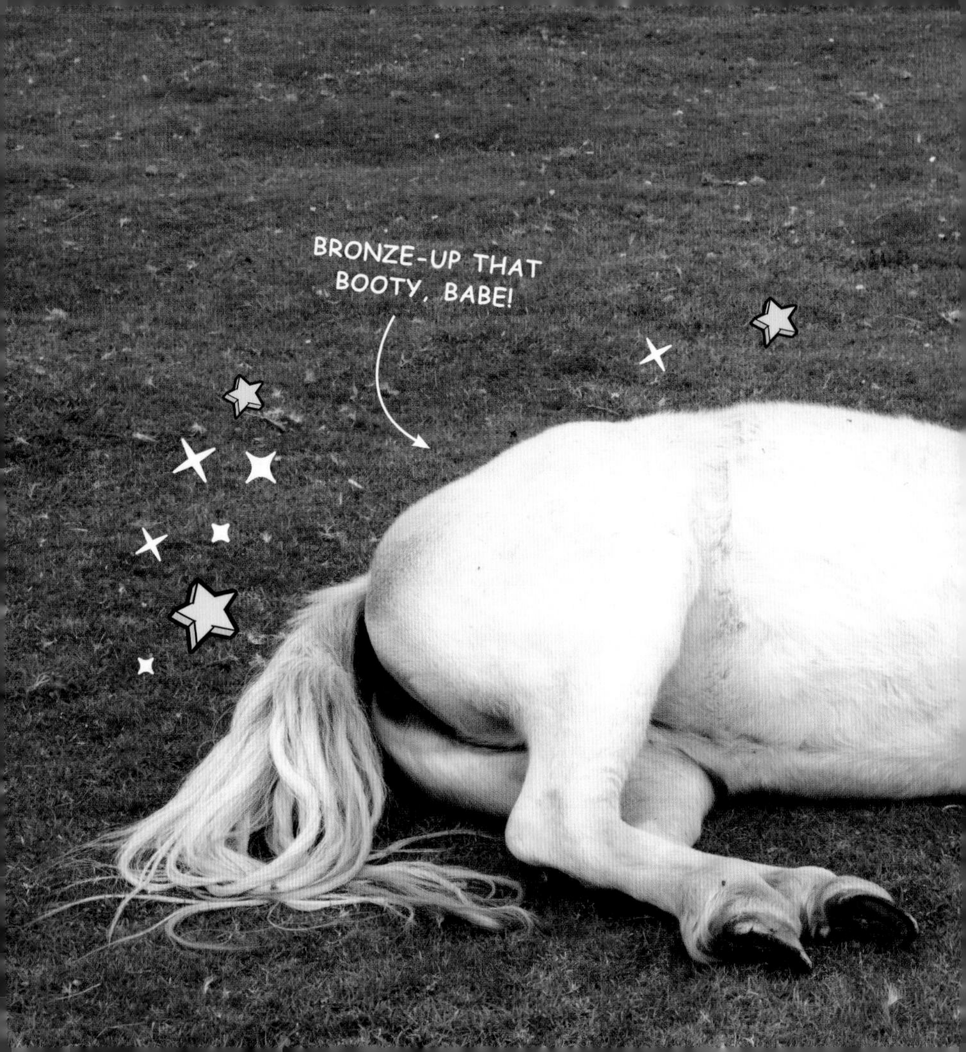
BRONZE-UP THAT BOOTY, BABE!

I MAY LOOK CUTE, BUT THIS IS SNOW CAMO SPECIALLY DESIGNED FOR SPARKLE-DIVISION MISSIONS. I COULD KILL YOU WITH ONE EYELASH.

SMOL DOGGO
ASSISTANT

HELL NO, BEING A GOTH IS NOT A PHASE...

Say anything and I'll be wearing YOU for a hat!
SNIGGERS
SNIGGERS

Oh, so you love unicorns but you couldn't care less when it's a unipony, could you?

SMOL BUT MIGHTY

TWINKLE TOES

INTERNAL SCREAMING

REALITY

BUTT OUTTA MY FACE, MAN!

HOW RUDE!

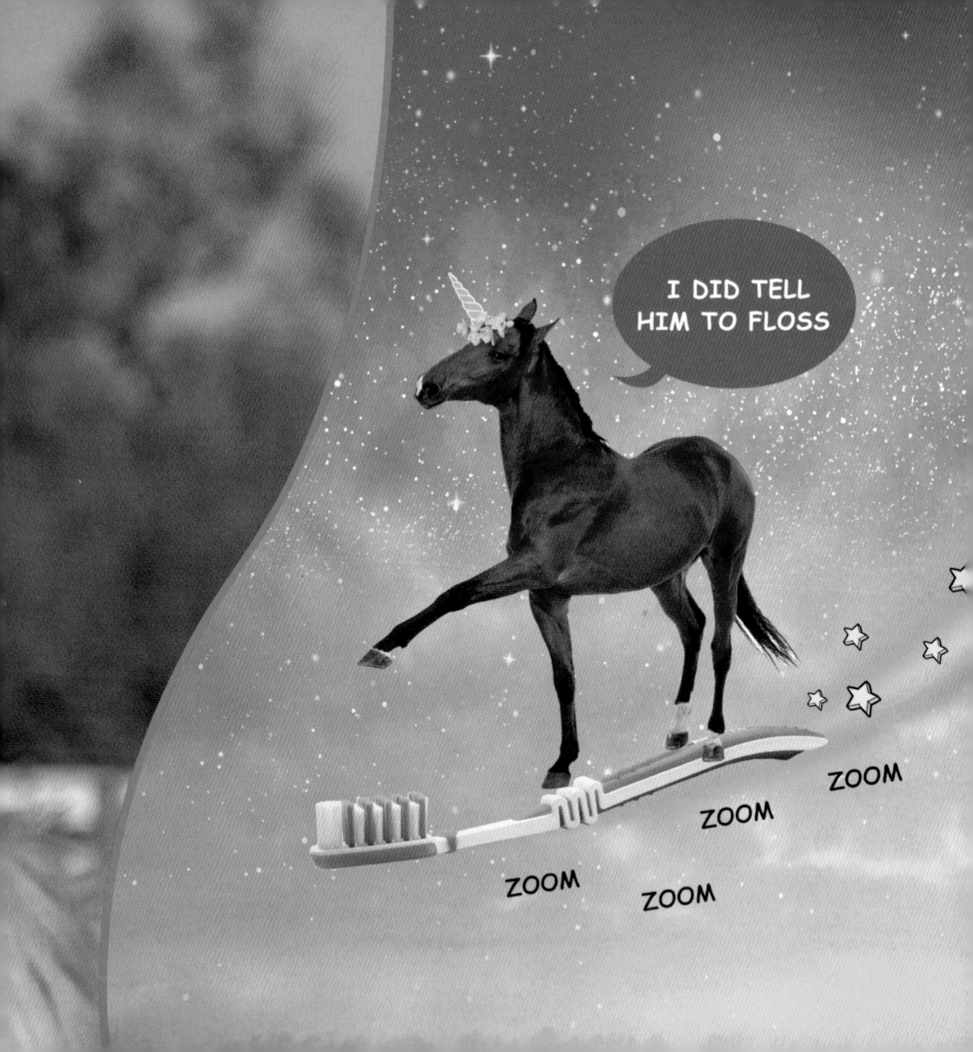
I DID TELL HIM TO FLOSS
ZOOM
ZOOM
ZOOM
ZOOM

Sugar's bad, carbs are bad,
fat is bad, meat is bad...

**all that's left is this
disgusting grass!**

Image credits

If you're interested in finding out more about our books, find us on Facebook at Summersdale Publishers and follow us on Twitter at @Summersdale.

www.summersdale.com